MISSION CHAMPIONISM

BITE-SIZED DOSES OF MUSINGS AND THOUGHTS TO INSPIRE YOU TO BE A CHAMPION AND BEHAVE LIKE ONE

DR. VIJAYAKUMAAR SRINIVASAN &
ARUNA VIJAYAKUMAAR SRINIVASAN

Made with ♥ on the Notion Press Platform
www.notionpress.com

This book is dedicated to each and every soul we have crossed in our journey thus far - the good ones, the not so good ones, the inspiring ones, the supportive ones, and all those who have been rooting for us all this while.

Vijay and Aruna

Contents

Contents

Contents

Foreword

Championism as a Science and an Art...

Championism is both a science and an art at the same time.

As a science, we can dissect it, fix formulae to acquire it, can learn by emulating other leaders and so on.

As an art, it is in-born, it is a philosophy, it blossoms from the mind and blooms into reality.

Whether it is a science or an art, the focal points of Success Mantra of Champions in their Personal Life are common. They are:

- Internalized positivity
- Contagious cheerfulness
- Respect for others' time
- Love-fired relationships
- Small group of 3-4 "non-toxic" friends
- Quality time for the "immediate" family
- Passion to learn from everybody
- Discipline in daily chores
- Determination to excel (fire-in-the-belly)
- Unflinching Faith in a Super Power

Others might misunderstand some of these traits as arrogance, but the Leaders/Champions carry on with their zeal to optimise their performance and continue in their journey to the zenith of glory.

Be a CHAMPION. Behave like a CHAMPION.

Prologue

Until a few years back, the Reader's Digest magazine used to state its philosophy as under:

> *"Articles of enduring significance in permanent, condensed, booklet form "*

We are inspired by that USP (Unique Selling Proposition) of Reader's Digest that we want to bring to you

"concepts of enduring significance in permanent, condensed, electronic form."

But if at times you find that we are over simplifying huge subjects, blame it on us.

If a chapter is on a worn-out subject, blame it on us.

If a chapter is a little long, blame it on us.

If a chapter is irreverent, blame it on us.

But if the post is short, remember these wonderful words of Oliver Goldsmith in his famous poem,

"An Elegy on the Death of a Mad Dog":

> *"Good people all of every sort*
> *Give ear unto my song*
> *And if you find it wonderous short*
> *It cannot hold you long"*

ONE

PB SHELLEY & TS ELLIOT

Although in our conversations, we have quoted liberally from Yeats to Keats, from HW Longfellow to HW Davies, from Goldsmith to Wordsworth, from Milton to Frost, our two most favourite poets are P.B. Shelley and T.S. Elliot.

One walked this planet in 19th century and the other in the 20th.

How many of us know that Leo Tolstoy, Karl Marx and Mahatma Gandhi were all influenced by Shelley's writings on nonviolent resistance?

Yes, Shelley's poetry always had a dose of radical idealism and he was forthright in his POVs on political and social issues. He was denied fame during his lifetime as readers avoided his writing for fear of being arrested for blasphemy or sedition. But recognition for his poetry grew steadily after his death. He said in the 1800s:

> "*"Gold is a living God and rules in scorn, All earthly things but Virtue." and*
>
> *"The encomium of one incapable of flattery is indeed flattering."*"

And who can forget his positive affirmation

“"IF WINTER COMES CAN SPRING BE FAR BEHIND?"”

Elliot is comparatively a recent era poet (1888 - 1965) and is hailed as the heralder of the modernist movement. A Nobel Prize winner, Elliot made himself immortal with his verse drama, "Murder in the Cathedral", that portrayed the opposition to authority by the protagonist, Archbishop Beckett. The assassination of Beckett actually happened in 1910 and Elliot wrote his play in 1935, based on the real-life incident with the help of an eye witness. The play is believed to be staged even today somewhere in the UK and was made into a successful Hollywood movie too.

> *“"Destiny waits in the hands of God, not in the hands of statesmen."”*

T.S. Elliot wrote these indelible lines in that play.

What a forethought?!

Another quote of his that we love is,

> *“"Only those who will risk going too far can possibly find out how far one can go."”*

We can consciously bring up such personalities who inspire us in our day-to-day thoughts and conversations. From Kamban to Kannadasan, from Covey to Senge, from Shakespeare to Shelley.

The reason is that words of such legends steer us towards CHAMPIONISM, reminding us that we too can make our lives sublime.

Let's take a moment now to reflect on the names of such powerful people that come to your mind - those who have left imprints of their traits for us to absorb and emulate.

TWO

ZEN AND THE ART OF CHAMPIONISM

This Topic is a two-fold elucidation of Zen and its impact on championism.

One is on effortless excellence and the other is on a typical 'zennish' way of living the moment.

Zen has an equal reputation of being a great philosophy and also a confusing practice.

Zen can never be understood but only felt and realised.

Zen Philosophy is unfolded with exercises like meditation, breathing, slow-moving-dance rituals, martial arts judo, karate and even weaponry like Kyudo, supposed to be a form of archery.

In one way, Zen teaches us how, through years of practice, an activity becomes effortless both mentally and physically, as if without a conscious control from the mind.

This is something that cannot be obtained even by a progressive study of the human action.

The analogy that Zen draws is that of a skilled and trained archer.

When engaged in hitting the bull's eye, the archer ceases to be conscious of herself/himself, and becomes one with the very act itself. This would be the heights of effortlessness, which we can identify when a Champion is "IN THE ZONE."

The second important teaching of Zen is "living in the present."

We all know that we must eat when we are hungry, we must lie down when we are sleepy and so on.

But Zen teaches us this a tad differently.

Eat when you eat.—

Sleep when you sleep.--

Dance when you dance.--

Talk when you talk.

The inner meaning to the statements above is that we must 'Be in the moment,' when we are doing something. Normally, when we eat we also indulge in lot of chatting. When we are in the bath, we think of things to do. When we sleep, we hardly sleep immediately.

Zen tells us that when we take a bath, experience the act of bathing.

Experience the experience of experiencing the bath.

Experience the experience of experiencing the experience.

According to legendary Zen monks, speaking of Zen and trying to explain Zen itself is a betrayal of Zen.

Excellence though Effortlessness and Being in the Present are two fundamental lessons from Zen for the Leaders/Champions out there in the world.

Zen teaches one to "BE IN THE PRESENT AND BE AT PEACE WITH ONESELF." Zen is a state of suspending all judgemental thinking and dropping all ideas, words, images and thoughts without getting involved in them.

There are several activities under the Zen Philosophy like Zazen Meditation, Koan Introspection, Zuisokukan Breathing, Shikantaza, etc.

The most important and interesting part of Zen is the plethora of one-liners which are so deep and pregnant with meaning but sometimes difficult to comprehend.

Here are a few Zen statements (translated loosely):

=========

Shouting never helps. It is rain that grows plants not thunder.

=======

Life gives possibility, not guarantee.

=======

Smoke and fire come together but only one of them makes us warm.

=======

If you are more fortunate than others, build a longer table not a taller fence.

========

Don't say NO. Go with the FLOW.

========

Learn from past.
Plan for future.
LIVE the present.

========

If you manipulate words, it is a lie.
If you play on words, it is humour.
If you hang onto words, it is bad.
If you transcend words, WISDOM it is.

========

Zen teaches us to be mindful of our inner self, be aware of the outer world and be present in the present.

Isn't this a distinct quality of a Champion?

Be a CHAMPION.

Behave like a CHAMPION.

THREE

TRUST

Placing TRUST on people around us is one of the spiritual laws of success, we would say.

TRUST starts with T which itself stands for TRUST.

Which means we must first start 'Trusting' others before expecting others to 'Trust' us.

So, let us 'T'rust people. Without 'T' we will only RUST.

FOUR

RESILIENCE

Losers fall once and do not get up at all.

Ordinary people fall 7 times and get up 3 times.

Successful people fall 7 times and get up 6 times.

Champions fall 7 times and get up 8 times.

Yes.

Champions are always a step ahead of the rest of the pack.

Resilience is their hallmark.

Failure to them is not a setback but a phase of their journey to glory.

Be a CHAMPION . Behave like a CHAMPION .

FIVE

4G

4G is very critical in today's use of telecom technology. For our everyday life too, we need 4G

but altogether from a lateral perspective:

- Gita
- Ganga
- Gayatri
- Govinda.

Reading the Gita.

A Dip in the Ganga.

Uttering the Gayatri mantra.

Chanting Govinda namah.

Each of these four gives us solace and strength; peace and power; agility and ability.

And needless to say, each of them can lead us to the 5th G, GOD

(Inspired by the verse "Bagavath Gita Kinchita Jeetha" from Bhaja Govindham, where Adi Sankara mentions the first 2Gs).

SIX

LEADERSHIP AND CHAMPIONISM

Leader and a Champion.

We are often asked a typical question: "What is the difference between a Leader and a Champion"?

Our answer has been consistent...

"Absolutely no difference.

It is their primary spectrum of activity/performance that separates them.

In normal parlance, a Leader operates in a corporate field while a Champion performs in sports, arts, home, spiritual field and so on and so forth.

"Every Leader is a Champion and every Champion is a Leader including homemakers, small entrepreneurs, students and anyone else.

Vision, Thinking, Attitude, Behaviour . . . . Nothing separates them."

Let's take a look at a few behavioural points.

Leaders NEVER face a conflict with fear.

Leaders NEVER fake a compliment with flattery.

Leaders NEVER fawn a relationship with favours.

Leaders NEVER flood a doubt with data.

Leaders NEVER fend a criticism with anger.

Leaders NEVER dilute discipline with irrelevant activities.

Don't these statements apply equally to Champions?

Leaders / Champions never miss an opportunity to optimize their contribution in order to maximize the end result.

Be a CHAMPION. Behave like a CHAMPION.

SEVEN

ETERNAL BLISS

Eternal Bliss.

> "*Yogarathova Bhogarathova*
> *sankarathova Sankaviheenaha*
> *Yasyaprammani ramate chitham*
> *nandathi nandathi nandathiyeva*
> *(Adishankarar)*"

Whether one is in yoga or is in boga,
Whether one lives amidst people or away from people,
One who revels with his inner self (Bramman),
His life will be dance, dance and nothing but dance.

The same concept finds place in the words of SIVA VAKIYA SITHAR sung in 10 AD:

> "*"Odi Odi Odi Odi utkalantha jothiyai*
> *Nadi nadi nadi nadi natkalum kazhindhu poi*
> *Vadi vadi vadi vadi vazhndhu pona maandhargal*
> *Kodi kodi kodi kodi ennirantha kodiye"*
> *(Siva Vaakkiyar)*"

The Eternal Bliss is what we search outside of us.

That is the "Pure Potentiality", as Deepak Chopra, the author of books like "Ageless Body Timeless Mind" calls.

This Eternal Bliss is nothing but ‘happiness’.

Happiness comes from within.

Joy comes from within.

Bliss comes from within.

Let’s revel in it. Let’s rejoice over it.

EIGHT

RED HOT PRINCIPLE

A lot of Philosophers and Management authors have drawn profusely from our Vedas, Upanishads etc.

Here goes one example.

Our Vedanta lays down how a good teacher must act when it comes to disciplining the students. It says the teacher should behave like fire.

The fire operates on 4 defining principles:

- 1. There is a forewarning
- 2. The burn is immediate
- 3. It is consistent
- 4. It is impartial.

A fire gives a forewarning that if anyone touches it, he/she would get burnt.

The person would get burnt immediately. Any number of times the person touches it, he/she would get burnt every time.

Irrespective of sex, caste, creed and status, everyone who touches fire would be burnt.

What a wonderful way of laying down a huge philosophy with a simple analogy.

Many authors drew inspiration from this and in particular, Douglas McGregor, the exponent of Motivation Theory, uses the concept of 'Red-hot Stove' to explain how an organization has to formulate its disciplinary policy and procedures therein.

He enlists the aforesaid 4 principles of Fire in the same order to explain his Red-hot Stove concept.

These guiding principles have been successfully applied in corporates not only for discipline but also for 'rewards' policy, and can also be effectively applied at home by parents in the upbringing of children.

NINE

HABIT

HABIT is a pure potential tool that God has blessed us all with.

It is a biogenic trait that one practices throughout one's life and it is so powerful that it drives us and conditions our behaviour.

Once formed, a HABIT, whether a good one or a bad one, becomes extremely difficult to get rid of.

If you drop H from it, ABIT (a bit) will remain.

If you drop A also from it, BIT will remain.

If you drop B too from it, IT will remain.

IT will remain at all times until we drop the "I', which is ego, and once we drop the I,

Only T will remain which can be swallowed because T (tea) is a beverage.

So, all the more imperative that we form only good habits.

And this applies even more to children in their formative years.

As proved scientifically, anything that is done 21 times will set as a HABIT.

Our Hindu Vedanta also says that anything that's heard or recited continuously for 21 times, will get registered in the mind and will stay with us.

And that's how, our over-5000 -year-old Holy Vedas have been handed down generation after generation.

TEN

PROCESS OF LEARNING

“"Learning is not the filling of a pail but the lighting of a flame,"”

said W B Yeats.

Thiruvalluvar says

““ karka kasadara””

Learning is a continuous process and irrespective of our age, the learning from our experience conditions our thinking, behaviour and more importantly our attitude.

Abdul Kalam famously said

“"Our Attitude determines our Altitude".”

We would add one more and say

“"Our Attitude and our Aptitude determine our Altitude".”

And all three are truly a resultant effect of our learning.

Avvaiyar, the golden lady who was larger than her legend, stated that there are 6 types of learners:

> "*1. The Leaky Pot - Whatever goes in goes out*
>
> *2. The Buffalo - Confuses oneself and spoils the place one is in (pond)*
>
> *3. The Goat - Surface grazer. Never does deep learning.*
>
> *4. The Parrot - This learner simply repeats what was learnt last*
>
> *5. The Sieve - Such people allow all the good things to pass and retain the bad unwanted ones just like a typical sieve.*
>
> *6. The Swan - As does a swan separate milk and water, this type of learners absorb all the good things while leaving out the unwanted.*"

Needless to say, you know what type of learner is a true CHAMPION.

Be a CHAMPION. Behave like a CHAMPION.

ELEVEN

CHAMPIONISM AND STARBUCKS

Starbucks is today the most successful and most popular coffeehouse chain from Seattle to Singapore, from Dubai to Detroit, from Bangalore to Boston and from Beijing to Bangkok.

Starbucks offers the SAME quality of coffee and the SAME quality of service at every outlet consistently.

You can walk into any Starbucks coffeehouse and ask for your double-tall-nonfat-mocha-with-a-little-vanilla-at-the-bottom----- and so on, and you will be served what you exactly ordered with an infectious smile.

Custom-brewed-coffee, home-grown-ingenuity and people-driven-philosophies have made Starbucks a huge success story.

Founded in 1971, the company operates in over 20,000 locations and employs over 200,000 'partners,' and their stocks have shown a steady staggering growth over the years.

The big question is HOW?

Every Starbucks partner (that's how they call their employees) is given a pocket-sized "Green Apron Book" that puts into words the core 'ways of being' that have to be steadfastly adhered to.

They are:

- Be Welcoming;

- Be Genuine;
- Be Knowledgeable;
- Be Considerate; and
- Be Involved.

These are simple words but they distill everything one needs to know about Starbucks and the people who work there. The partners live the word, walk the talk and keep the Starbucks flag flying at hi-mast at all times and at all places.

Aren't the governing principles of Starbucks equally applicable at the home front and if we do follow them to the letter T, can excellence in our relationships be in doubt at all?

Let's ponder over.

TWELVE
MEDITATION

What is meditation?

I want to share what I learnt in my Leadership Training I attended way back in 1992 in Japan and later at Osho camp in Pune.

(As most of you know, I have been a practitioner and trainer of meditation for 20+ years).

Let us start with what happens in sleep.

During sleep, 4 conditions occur:

- 1. There is almost nil organic activity
- 2. Body temperature comes down
- 3. Blood circulation slows down
- 4. Breathing becomes even.

And so, we feel refreshed after a good sleep.

In Meditation, all these 4 conditions are 'made' to happen without us falling asleep.

And that's why we feel recharged after a nice spell of meditation.

Meditation is not a thought-less state but it is "being with our thoughts."

It is not concentrating on something, which is Dharana.

The Sanskrit word 'Dhyana' means Na Dhya, meaning 'doing nothing.'

Chinmayananda says it beautifully "Be at Peace with whatever is" while elucidating the 8 limbs of yoga called "Ashtanga Yoga,"

Rishi Patanjali mentions DHARANA as the 6th step,

DHYANA as the 7th step and SAMADHI (Thoughtlessness) as the 8th step.

So, let's just shut out distractions (sit in a calm place, close our eyes), be with our thoughts whatever they may be, be still and silent and meditation shall HAPPEN.

It is as simple as that.

THIRTEEN

LOVE

ThiruGnanasambandhar says

> " *"kadhalagi kasindhu kanneer malgi"* "

And feels prayer itself is Love.

Prayer in action is Love.

Love in action is compassion.

Love is not about possession. Love is about sharing.

Love is not about correction. Love is about appreciation.

Love is not a tool. It's an emotion.

Love is not a technique. It's a feeling.

Love propels us to see the invisible, feel the intangible and accomplish the impossible.

Falling in love we remain a child.

Rising in love we become enlightened.

We should seek to grow in love so that, at some stage

We are not in love; we have not fallen in love; we are not rising in love;

We ARE Love.

FOURTEEN

PRAYERS

Putting DAYS into our LIFE is ageing.

Putting LIFE into our DAYS is LIVING.

Ageing is inevitable. Living is a choice.

Experience is inevitable. Learning is a choice.

Karma is inevitable. Faith is a choice.

Problem is inevitable. Prayer is a choice.

Experience creates confusion. Learning clears it.

Karma creates fear. Faith nullifies it.

Problem creates worry. Prayer dissolves it.

Have belief in Prayer. Have faith in Prayer.

Prayer gives . .

Peace to our past

Purpose to our present and

Potence to our future.

We have been associated with suicide-prevention by volunteering for a social organization for the past several years and we have worked with teenagers and drug addicts. During that experience, we came across the Alcoholic Anonymous group.

The AA movement has been doing a fine job of helping addicts to overcome their weakness through a simple process of confession and that too without any coercion.

Their approach would come under "Collective Wisdom" which helps the members.

The premise is "Never let your strength weaken a bit and never let your weakness strengthen a bit."

Their prayer, the original credited to Christopher Reinhold Niebuhr, runs like this:

> “*"God, give me the serenity to accept what I cannot change;*
> *The courage to change what I ought to change;*
> *And the wisdom to know the difference between the two."*”

What a wonderful prayer, isn’t it?

If we can internalize the essence of this, our distress about the past,

Uncertainties of the present and doubts about the future will all be dissolved like a Koan puzzle.

Our regular prayer has been a ’thank you' God and an adaptation of the AA prayer.

"God, I realise my responsibilities. Give me the ability to fulfil them."

What are your prayers?

FIFTEEN
COMPETENCE

Warren Buffett, the most successful investor in the planet says that there are 2 circles defining our competence.

> *"An outer and an inner circle."*

The inner circle depicts "What we actually know " and the outer circle depicts "What we THINK we know." And if we genuinely studied our competence level in this manner, it can be a little depressing.

We believe there are 4 stages of Competence

- 1. Unconscious Incompetence
- 2. Conscious Incompetence
- 3. Unconscious Competence
- 4. Conscious Competence

All 4 stages are important in the spectrum of life and in the development of our mental faculty.

Unconscious Incompetence

This is "I don't know and I don't know that I don't know."

I am blind and in a State of ignorance which itself can be a blissful experience and many a time, ignorance can save us.

Conscious Incompetence

This is "I don't know but I know that I don't know." Learning starts from this stage. Awareness, acknowledgement and acceptance of what I don't know will help me to acquire knowledge.

Unconscious Competence

This is "I may know but I don't know that I know." Remember Anjaneya who had to be reminded of his prowess. Once their true potential is realised, what will be unleashed is sheer prolific performance.

Conscious Competence

This is "I know and I know that I know."

Humility resonates with excellence in this stage.

Mastery and modesty together take a walk in the park.

Sachin Tendulkar, Roger Federer, AR Rahman and such legends belong here.

In every aspect of our life we all knowingly and unknowingly move up the ladder and

Champions reach the pinnacle a little faster.

Be a CHAMPION. Behave like a CHAMPION.

SIXTEEN

NAVA VIDHA BHAKTI

Srimad Bagavadham elucidates the nine types of Bakthi called Nava Vidha bakthi to demonstrate devotion to God.

> "*Shravanam Keerthanam Vishnu:*
> *Smaranam padhasevanam*
> *archanam vandhanam dhasyam*
> *saakyam atmanivedhanam.*
> *7.5.23*"

We totally believe in Servant-Leadership (coined by Robert Greenleaf).

It is a concept where the Leader functions as if he is there to Serve his people and not to order his people around. Our take is that a true servant-leader HAS to follow all the above 9 ways towards his people in the organization, albeit, not as Bakthi but as ways of 'relating' with his people.

1. Shravanam - Responsive Listening to the people
2. Keerthanam - Spontaneous Singing of their contribution
3. Smaranam - Always thinking about them
4. Padha Sevanam - Service mindedness
5. Archanam - Praising their qualities and attributes
6. Vandanam - Showing Undiluted Respect for everyone
7. Dhasyam - "Anything-for-my-people" attitude

8. Sakhyam - Absolute friendliness living up to the Kural

> "*udukkai izhandhavan kai pola aange*
> *idukkan kalaivatham natpu.*"

9. Atma Nivedhanam - Unconditional surrender to the welfare of the people

Again, needless to say, the aforesaid 9 paths will help us to a great deal not only in the professional life but in personal one too.

SEVENTEEN

3D

If one is unwelcome wherever one goes, one is worthless.

If one is tolerated wherever one goes, one is a mediocre.

If one is accepted wherever one goes, one is a nice person.

If one is celebrated wherever one goes, one is a CHAMPION.

This is so because Champions make EXCELLENCE a passion, a way of life and the journey to success.

They reach the zenith of glory through sheer performance marked by the 3Ds

- Dedication,
- Determination and
- Discipline.

Their compassion despite their problems, and their humility despite their accomplishments stand out in prominence.

Be a CHAMPION. Behave like a CHAMPION.

EIGHTEEN

SIX THINKING HATS BY EDWARD DE BONO

Edward de Bono - the very name is synonymous with Creativity and the concept of Lateral Thinking.

Vijay had the opportunity to attend a workshop personally facilitated by him about 15 years back in the US and it was a wonderful learning platform. Vijay also had the privilege of being part of an exclusive 8-member group for a breakfast-chat with the gr8 man. And that was a very fulfilling experience.

de Bono's 6 Thinking Hats are a set of extremely useful tools for us.

He writes in his book of the same title how we can accentuate our thinking by wearing or pretending to wear a HAT of a specific colour and thereby adapting a different style for different situations.

The different hats and their respective roles:

- WHITE HAT Wear it to get an objective look at data and information

- RED HAT Wear it to demonstrate feelings, hunches and intuition.
- BLACK HAT Wear it for logical-negative opinion, judgement and caution
- YELLOW HAT Wear it for logical-positive thinking, feasibility and benefits
- GREEN HAT Wear it to give new ideas and to offer creativity
- BLUE HAT Wear it to control the very process of thinking including which hat to wear

The method may seem extremely simple and even childish - but it works. The visualisation of the hats and their colours help to maximize results with minimised efforts. It is a great tool in parallel-thinking.

The technique is not person-related but it is situation-oriented. It helps an individual to get clarity on what decision to make. It helps a group (as in a corporate meeting) with collaborative exploration.

For instance, if Yellow hat is worn by all, then everyone makes an effort to find points of value and benefits in the suggestion, even if one dislikes the suggestion.

We have worn the White, Red, Yellow and Blue hats in the reverse sequence to write this chapter.

Which hat/s are you going to wear to dissect this book?

NINETEEN

SPREZZATURA

It's an Italian word - the dictionary meaning of SPREZZATURA is "Gracefulness without any apparent effort."

To us, Sprezzatura is "Effortless Excellence."

And this in our view, is what differentiates a true CHAMPION from the other run-of-the-mill performers.

Excellence-centric performance -- Results-centric Excellence

Excellence-centric Positivity --Discipline-centric Excellence

Excellence-centric Passion and Humility-centric Excellence

These are the true hallmarks of champions and are there for everyone to see. But an EFFORTLESS ELEGANCE sparkles through every movement of these wonderful Champions and is not noticed by everyone.

And that's SPREZZATURA.

Examples of 'sprezzaturas' who come to mind are Sachin, Federer, Schumacher, Steve Jobs, Bill Gates, our own Narayanamoorthi, the Late Abdul Kalam and many others.

The common thread that links these leaders is "Effortless Excellence", otherwise called Sprezzatura.

Isn't each of them an inspiration to their own generation and to all the coming ones?

We are both Toyota fanatics, yes, fanatics.

To us, Toyota fits the "Sprezzatura" quality to the letter T as a corporate entity.

There are many more companies (GE, Honda, Apple, Microsoft, J&J, Google etc) but Toyota is close to my heart.

Toyota is an impact player. It is one of the market leaders in hybrid vehicles (Prius is a standing and outstanding example). Started in 1937, the Japanese giant is today the 2nd largest automotive manufacturer in the world behind the German Volkswagen. Apart from the Toyota brand itself, they have 4 other brands Hino, Lexus, Ranz, Daihatsu and all have stood the test of time and have been the numero uno in their respective category at some point of time.

Toyota proudly says that their quality of products and quality of people have given them this status.

The organization has a saying, "mono zukuri was Hi to zukuri" which means "making things is about making people." Another famous expression heard in Toyota is "We don't just build cars; we build people."

In our minds the Success Mantra of TOYOTA that makes them a Sprezzatura are:

1. Niche business strategy
2. Fair-profit-conscience player
3. Bold creativity
4. Sustained R&D
5. Customer-First execution
6. Balanced people orientation
7. Perfection driven Quality
8. Energy-filled aggressive marketing .

There may be an organization that demonstrates one or two qualities but Toyota is the only company that practices all of the above.

Every Toyota manager doubles up as a teacher teaching the above principles to the people.

Toyota is purely my choice and the aforesaid qualities differentiate them from others.

We would love to hear about your Sprezzatura company and a few qualities that keep them above the others.

TWENTY

STEPHEN COVEY

Stephen Covey's magnum opus "The Seven Habits of Highly Effective People" revolutionised management thinking especially at the personal level.

The paradigm shift that many corporates and leaders had after following the Covey concepts has become folkloric. We believe that his greatest contribution is in the area of Time Management.

Covey says that the very concept Time management is a misnomer.

No one can 'manage' time. One can only manage the events or activities.

Time Management is not just about being punctual. It is about valuing our own time and much more about valuing others' time.

Covey gives us a Principle-Centered approach called "FIRST THINGS FIRST."

It's a simplistic way saying "the main thing is to keep the main thing the main thing."

Covey insists on prioritising our events and activities because

Activity is time-flexible and Time is quantum-specific.

Covey suggests that we prioritize our activities into Vital, Important and Optional.

And then further categorize them into 4 quadrants as detailed below in the order Q1, Q3, Q4 and the all-important Q2.

He basically uses the combo of 4 states, Important, Not important, Urgent and Not Urgent.

Quadrant I -

Important and Urgent

All activities that are pressing problems, deadline driven and have already become crises.

(Last date for paying the electricity bills). We HAVE to just do these things.

Quadrant III -

Urgent Not important

Interruptions, popular activities, phone calls etc.

Activities that we do immediately but that are not important.

We do these things but we CAN avoid them if we choose to.

Quadrant IV -

Not important not urgent.

Trivia, time wasters, whiling away. Sheer spoilers.

Time saved from not doing these can be used for carrying out activities in other quadrants.

Quadrant II -

Important not urgent

The Quadrant to operate from.

Marked by Planning, Preventing, Preparation, etc. (Planning for the wedding of a child years ahead.

Preparations for a Board presentation a few weeks in advance).

While we HAVE to do these things, they CAN be taken up a little later.

Of course, if we push the clock too much, they will move to Q I, which will be pretty bad.

Q I activities may look like "cannot-be-avoided" kind of things, but if we plan to do them well ahead of the deadline, they move to Q II.

The other two Quadrants are much easier to get out of.

So, let's put First Things FIRST and operate from Quadrant II,

the epicentre of Principle Centered Living, which is what a CHAMPION does.

TWENTY-ONE

COMMUNICATION

Communication has been the most vital of all the work-skills all these years and today psychologists emphasize that it is an important life-skill too.

Communication is all about context, content, clarity, coherence and style.

Although it includes a variety of spectrums like oral, written, non-verbal and listening,

Today we will take a lighter look at verbal communication.

(We will take up Listening and other aspects of communication later).

Some people 'think' they know what to say.

Some people 'know' what to say.

Some people know what to say and 'how' to say.

Some people know what to say, how to say and 'when' to say

Some people know what to say, how to say, when to say and 'where' to say.

Some people know what to say, how to say, when to say, where to say and 'whom' to say.

Leaders/Champions not only know what to say, how to say, when to say, where to say, whom to say but are also totally clear "WHETHER" to say it or not.

BE a Champion. BEHAVE like a Champion.

TWENTY-TWO

ANDHAADHI

This is a form of poetry wherein the last word
Of the first line forms the first word of the second line
Which is followed for the whole poem. This is popular in Tamil.
Frails are mine. Hails are for English.
======
In any situation, Leaders / Champions .
Understand more than what they perceive.
Perceive more than what they observe.
Observe more than what they see.
See more than what they look.
Be a CHAMPION. Behave like a CHAMPION.

TWENTY-THREE

A.I.M.

Viijay used to do a series of leadership programmes called "A I M," which he did for many corporates for GMs, VPs and other senior executives. Simultaneously, he used to do an adapted version for the spouses of such executives. Here is a synopsis.

A I M: Align. Improve. Manage.

(Each had 3 modules plus 1 Intro and 1 Concluding modules).

ALIGN --

Align your goals. Align your people's/children's goals. Align their contributions. Align all of these with the organization/family goals.

IMPROVE --

Improve your capabilities. Improve your people's/children's ideas. Improve your contribution to their ideas and actions.

MANAGE --

Manage people/children/relatives. Manage process. Manage competition. Manage discipline and rewards mechanism (remember the Redhot Stove concept).

Champions AIM to think high.

Champions AIM to achieve big.

Champions AIM to inspire others.

TWENTY-FOUR

DYNAMIC MEDITATION

Time to understand Dynamic Meditation, the form that we have learnt, practised and administered to many people for 15-20 years now.

Although many of the exercises find a mention in age-old yoga sutras of India, it is the Chinese and Japanese who have popularised it in its current form.

We do hope you remember the 4 conditions of sleep that we voluntarily make happen in meditation, namely, Nil organic activity, Reducing body temperature, Slowing down blood circulation and Regulated breathing.

In Dynamic Meditation we create the exact opposite of the above conditions,

1. Perform an organic activity
2. Thereby Increasing body temperature
3. Which makes the blood circulation faster and
4. Because of all of these, making our breathing uneven.

When we do as shown above for a few minutes and put a stop, automatically all the 4 conditions needed for meditation set in smoothly.

It is akin to taking a pendulum to one extreme and releasing it, where the pendulum WILL go to the other end.

This action is called Goal-Directed Restlessness.

You intentionally climb a mountain of RESTLESSNESS and once you reach the peak. You move one step further, and fall into the valley of RESTFULNESS.

This is Dynamic Meditation.

Organic activity for a few minutes and stopped, followed by a spell of silence and stillness, letting meditation happen.

Brahmari, Gibberish, Yaahai-Yaahuk, Hollow Bamboo etc are some dynamic meditations.

If you are interested, here is a simple Dynamic Meditation exercise.

==================

Close your eyes.

Stuff both your ears with the forefingers as tightly as you can.

Make a buzzing sound like a bee for as long as you can.

Take a breather.

Continue to keep your eyes shut and ears stuffed.

Again, Make a buzzing sound like a bee.

Take a breather.

Yet again, Make a buzzing sound like a bee.

Keep doing so for 3 to 4 minutes.

And then Stop.

Be silent and still for 5 mts.

Gently remove your fingers from your ears.

Rub your hands together.

Slowly open your eyes looking into your palms.

=================

You have just learnt "Brahmari," the humming bee breathing, one of the most popular exercises in Dynamic Meditation.

TWENTY-FIVE

10 COMMANDMENTS OF CHAMPIONS

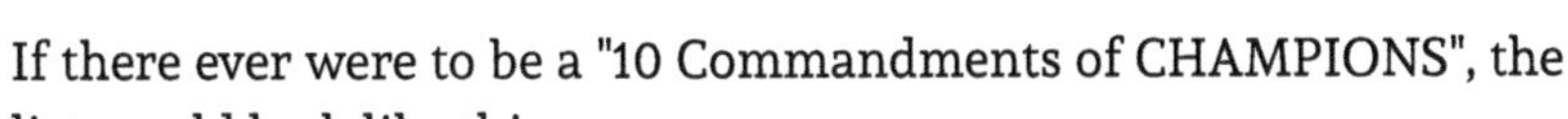

If there ever were to be a "10 Commandments of CHAMPIONS", the list would look like this:

1. Thou SHALT be creative yet be structured
2. Thou SHALT be self-reliant yet be interdependent
3. Thou SHALT be curious to learn yet be willing to unlearn
4. Thou SHALT be compassionate yet be assertive
5. Thou SHALT be proactive yet be restrained
6. Thou SHALT be ever relaxed yet be dynamic
7. Thou SHALT take calculated risks yet be rational
8. Thou SHALT be celebrative yet be responsive to others
9. Thou SHALT go the extra mile yet not be anxious about rewards
10. Thou SHALT be inspirational yet be humble.

We could see that every commandment states both sides of a coin in every behaviour aspect.

Obviously, true Sprezzaturas/Leaders/Champions have a balanced way of life, never sticking to one side of the pendulum but comfortably operating in the middle.

Be a CHAMPION. Behave like a CHAMPION.

TWENTY-SIX

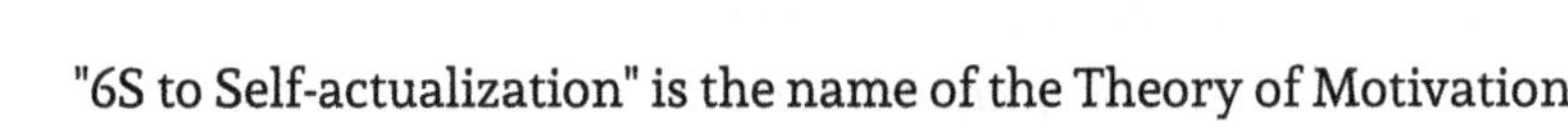

"6S to Self-actualization" is the name of the Theory of Motivation that Vijay had come up with as part of his PhD Thesis.

The management world basically has 6 theories of motivation:

- Hertzberg's Two-factor theory
- Maslow's Hierarchy of Needs
- McGregor' S Theory X and Y
- The Hawthorne Effect
- The Expectancy Theory and
- The 3-Dimensional theory of Attribution

All of them invariably trace how a human's needs flow from fundamental to self-satisfaction levels.

Each of the theories speak of the following in one way or other:

1. Identity/Security needs
2. Monetary/Safety needs
3. Support/Dependency needs
4. Rewards/Growth needs
5. Esteem/Self-Actualization needs

Adapting the above theories, we conceptualized our very own theory of motivation which states the 6 Stages of Needs to be crossed to reach the SELF-ACTUALIZATION, the pinnacle, as given below :

1st S : SURVIVAL

2nd S : SUSTENANCE

3rd S : STABILITY

4th S : STRENGTH

5th S : SUCCESS

6th S : SUPERIORITY

The 7th S will be SELF-ACTUALIZATION.

The 6 needs must be fulfilled and only then the the big S will be felt.

Every human being has the power of pure potentiality

to have obtained the 7th S in some spectrum of their lives.

It is the intrinsic satisfaction level that may not be displayed nor may it be visibly felt by others.

SELF-ACTUALIZATION as such is "anirvacaniya." Indescribable.

It cannot fit into any known pattern of human nature. And more so,

this very need differs from person to person based on the perspectives of each individual.

SELF-ACTUALIZATION is the ultimate self-fulfilment state,

the tendency for an individual to become actualized in what he or she is potentially strong.

This is the place a true LEADER/CHAMPION reaches faster than others in a chosen sphere of performance.

Let's identify in which stage of the needs are we at present in every aspect of our lives.

And if we have accomplished the 7th S, which most of you must have already achieved,

let's feel intrinsically proud.

Be a CHAMPION. Behave like a CHAMPION.

TWENTY-SEVEN

MEDITATION AND YOGA

We are often asked how meditation differs from yoga.

We believe Yoga conditions our body and Meditation conditions our mind.

Yoga makes our body supple and strong while Meditation makes our mind flexi and strong.

Both bring in restfulness and energy, calmness and agility.

Another way to look at the subject is to first understand Ashtanga Yoga

a step-by-step approach credited to Patanjali's Yoga Sutra,

although the saint never called it Ashtanga Yoga.

He only called it the 8 limbs of yoga which are . . . .

1. YAMA ---- Abstention from a set of specific things and activities

2. NIYAMA ---- Performing a set of must-do actions

3. ASANA ----- Posture - the way one has to sit, stand or perform an act

4. PRANAYAMA ----Regulating and controlling one's breathing

5. PRATYAHARA ---Removing attention from all material distractions

6. DHARANA ---Bringing all the focus to one object or sound of one's own choice

7. DHYANA ---Being with one's own thoughts

(Remember "Be at Peace with whatever is")

8. SAMADHI ------The ultimate. The real thoughtless state. The communion with divinity.

Our opinion is that of these 8 limbs,

Yoga focuses more on the first 4 limbs while

Meditation focuses more on the last 4 limbs.

The key words are "focuses more."

The two practices overlap each other in a seamless manner.

Nobody can substantiate that one is superior to the other.

TWENTY-EIGHT

KNOWLEDGE

The ladder of KNOWLEDGE is a very interesting subject and is perfectly pertinent to learning, which can happen at any age.

Whatever we do, we gain at least a grain of knowledge.

The ladder starts with Information and peaks with Wisdom in 6 steps. Here we go . . . .

INFORMATION

What we gather continuously is Information

- This is the stage of a Novice.

KNOWLEDGE

When we refine the information gathered and use what interests us, it becomes Knowledge.

- We are now an Advanced Beginner.

SKILL

When we apply your knowledge and transform it into action, we attain Skill.

- We not only know what to do, we also know how to do it and are now a Performer.

INSIGHT

As a performer if we know how to do, when to do what, why to do something in a particular way and why not in another way, we have got Insight in your skillset.

- We become a Contributor.

FORESIGHT

When we clearly understand how relevant our present skillset will be at a later date or in a different place, we are said to have gained Foresight.

- We are now an Expert.

WISDOM

When we cross the aforesaid 5 steps successfully, and apply all the knowledge gained in a Conscious Competence state, we become a person of Wisdom.

- The Master. The Teacher. The Learned.

The Hindu Vedanta says that we are at different stages of the ladder in different aspects of our capabilities and whatever STEP we are in, we become a teacher for those in the steps below us.

And there's a specific name for the assigned teacher for every step.

Mukophadhyaya gives Information.

Upadhyaya gives knowledge.

Acharya gives skills and knowledge.

Pandit gives insight, skills and knowledge.

Drishta gives foresight, insight, skills and knowledge.

Gnanaguru gives wisdom and everything else.

Whatever step we are in as a performer, we will be one level below as a teacher.

Need we state where does a champion stand as a performer and as a teacher?

Be a CHAMPION. Behave like a CHAMPION.

TWENTY-NINE

INTERDEPENDENCE

Interdependence is a concept popularised by Stephen Covey while explaining his "Win-win Syndrome."

One is not just dependant on another, each of us is interdependent.

Whether in a family or at school, in a community or at workplace,

it is only when people work together and for one another,

that the common good is attained.

No surprises. This also dates back to 1000s of years as this abstract idea

is mentioned in Baghavath Gita. (Ch III - 11)"

Parasparam bhavayantah sreyah param avapsyathe "--

By mutually enriching one another you will attain the highest good

"Enriching one another."

Even if one ignores the mythological dimensions, one can find in the Gita

pearls of wisdom of practical value for all times.

Indeed, each one of us is rich in different ways:

in material wealth, in intelligence, in our capabilities for kindness and love and so on.

Each time we use our resources for another person's benefit, we enrich ourselves because good goes around and comes back to us.

Cricket is a classic example of "parasparam bhavayantah" because

a batsman has to RUN for his partner too.

If a batsman hits and completes two runs, the other fellow has to RUN two too

but does not get anything added to his score.

The Australian cricket team used to have a simple advice for its cricketers: "Play for others."

That is Interdependence.

Champions always play for others as much as they play for themselves.

Be a CHAMPION. Behave like a CHAMPION.

THIRTY

RAMA AND KRISHNA - A STUDY

Let's for a change take a deep look at two divine CHAMPIONS, Rama and Krishna.

Unlike all the other avatars, these two are "POORNA" avatars.

Their valour, brilliance and "thejas" were unquestionably the most supreme. There ends the similarity.

In all other aspects they were poles apart:

1. RAMA - born in a palace but lived like a pauper

(in 'vanavasam' and was estranged from his wife too)

KRISHNA - born in a prison but lived like a king with a royal disposition

2. RAMA - never behaved like a divine power. Rarely displayed it.

KRISHNA - always behaved like God and even said So on many occasions.

3. RAMA - fought all his battles directly.

KRISHNA - killed a few asuras by hand but never took a weapon even in Kurukshetra.

4. RAMA - accepted a few people as brothers and Anjaneya as a dhasan.

KRISHNA - accepted a few people only as friends. None as brother or dhasan.

5. RAMA - helped and gave boons to quite a few without their asking.

KRISHNA - except Kusela, never helped or gave boons to anyone without their seeking His help.

6. RAMA - ஏகபத்தினி விரதனாய் வாழ்ந்தவன்.

KRISHNA - ஏகமாய் துணைவியர் அமைந்தவன்

.

7. RAMA - was a role-model, showed HOW to live like a man without advising others.

KRISHNA - was always on an advisory mode though He Himself lived a royal life.

8. RAMA - had an arranged marriage.

KRISHNA - .all his marriages (with Satyabama, Rukmini, Radha) were love marriages, purely arranged by Him.

9. RAMA - through out His avatar He was present only in one place at a time.

KRISHNA - was always omnipresent.

10. RAMA - தீயவரை அழித்து நல்லோரை காத்ததை சொல்லாமல் செய்தான்

KRISHNA - அதையே "பரித்ராணாய சாதூனாம்" என்று சொல்லிச் செய்தான்

11. RAMA - yielded to others' pressures on several occasions.

KRISHNA - nobody, and I say NOBODY, could ever put pressure on Him.

12. RAMA AVATAR was to show how God can live like a man.

KRISHNA AVATAR was to show how a man can live like a God.

The idea of today's post is to elucidate that Leaders/Champions can be made of qualities that are distinctly different between them.

THIRTY-ONE

VEDHAS

Human beings cannot survive without communicating with someone or other for something or other.

Whether it is oral or written, whether in person or through media, conversations fill our day.

Many times dialogues (vadhas) lead to arguments.

Though not all of them turn bitter, vadhas bring life to the relationship itself.

We have 4 types of vadhas.

The first is PLAIN Vadha.

This is a dialogue between equals.

What will emerge is a sense of belonging even if there is no conclusive end to the dialogue.

The second is JALPA Vadha.

The person indulging in Jalpa Vadha maintains the "I-am-right" stand.

He does not have time or the mind to listen to the other person's viewpoint.

He keeps harping on his own standpoint.

The dialogue dies a sudden death when the other person stops saying anything.

After it becomes a monologue, only the Jalpa person speaking.

The third is VIDHANDA Vadha.

The person displaying Vidhanda Vadha keeps putting down the other person with "no-no-you-are-wrong" approach.

He fills his argument with points that counter whatever the other person says.

A sense of bitterness will normally emerge even though the dialogue might continue more like a debate.

The fourth is SAM Vadha.

This is a dialogue between a guru and a sishya.

The teacher and a student always demonstrate a willingness to teach and a willingness to learn respectively. Ex., is the Krishna-Arjuna dialogue right at a battle field?

A Champion has less and less of Jalpa and Vidhanda Vadhas

and more and more of Plain and Sam Vadhas.

The champion knows when to get out of an argument and sometimes even when to stay away.

The Champion also knows when to teach and when to learn.

Be a CHAMPION. Behave like a CHAMPION.

THIRTY-TWO

LATERAL THINKING

LATERAL THINKING is a tool that many people stay away from, for the fear of getting things wrong.

It is a wonderful technique promulgated by Edward de Bono about nearly five decades back.

LATERAL THINKING gives us the ability to think creatively or "outside-the-box" through viewing things in a new and unusual light.

The approach uses reasoning and involves thinking of ideas beyond traditional step-by-step logic.

LATERAL THINKING can be learned, practiced and used by restructuring insight and by changing our impulsive perceptions.

Contrary to the belief, Lateral Thinking encompasses Logical reasoning and can stand any test for objective queries.

Let's try and solve a few of the problems given below.

If you solve even a few problems without any external help, you have learnt LATERAL THINKING.

1. What is the longest word in English?

2. At my favourite fruit shop an Orange costs Rs 18, a Pineapple costs Rs 27 and an Apple costs Rs 15. How much will a mango cost in that shop?

3. What is the next number in this series?

1248 1632 6412 8256 . . . .

4. A woman has two sons who were born on the same hour of the same day of the same year. But they are not twins. How could this be so?

5. The number 8,549,176,320 is the only one of its kind. What is so special about it?

6. How many Ts are there in the name Timothy Tuttle?

7. In India and in England and in the US, what occurs once in June and twice in August but never occurs in October?

8. What are the two missing numbers in the series below

43337__365

Happy solving.

THIRTY-THREE

LATERAL THINKING - ANSWERS

1. What is the longest word in English?

Smiles.

There is a "mile" between the first and the last letter.

2. At my favourite fruit shop an Orange costs Rs 18, a Pineapple costs Rs 27 and an Apple costs Rs 15. How much will a mango cost in that shop?

It is @Rs 3 per letter in the name of the fruit.

So a mango will cost Rs 15

3. What is the next number in this series?

1248 1632 6412 8256 . . . .

The answer is 5121.

It is going In the sequence 1, 2, 4, 8, 16, 32, 64, 128, 256. So the next will be 512 and 1024.

4. A woman has two sons who were born on the same hour of the same day of the same year. But they are not twins. How could this be so?

They are two of a triplet.

5. The number 8,549,176,320 is the only one of its kind. What is so special about it?

The digits zero to 9 are arranged in the alphabetical order.

6. How many Ts are there in the name Timothy Tuttle?

Only 2 Ts.

The other 't's are in the lower case.

7. In India and in England and in the US, what occurs once in June and twice in August but never occurs in October?

It is the alphabet U

8. What are the two missing numbers in the series below

43337__365

The number of letters in each word in the question are given in the series.

So the answer is 7 and 2, the letters in 'numbers' and 'in'

It really does not matter how many did you get right.

You are thinking out of the box.

You are experiencing LATERAL THINKING.

A ZEN statement to end this chapter on Lateral Thinking:

"We may be only a drop in the ocean.

But we are a whole ocean in the drop.

We may move only one stone now.

But ultimately we may shift the mountain."

THIRTY-FOUR

Japanese Tea Ceremony

CHANOYU or CHADO is the traditional Tea Ceremony of Japan where matcha, powdered green tea is used.

The same ceremony is called SENCHA, if tea leaves are used.

The Tea Ceremony act teaches us the following:

- how to gain subject-matter expertise,
- how to cultivate a willingness to learn a simple activity,
- how to be focused,
- how to remain in present,
- how to pay attention to details,
- how not to quit midway
- how to remain humble before the guest, and
- how to enjoy what you do.

These qualities are the guiding principles of Leaders/Champions.

To this day, we cannot think of a CHAMPION who doesn't adhere to even one of the above.

A clear differentiating factor, isn't it?

Champions might emulate someone else and still scale a taller peak with effortless elegance.

Leaders/Champions
never FAIL to sparkle,
never FAIL to arise to the occasion,

never FAIL to excel and
never FAIL to inspire.
Be a CHAMPION. Behave like a CHAMPION.

THIRTY-FIVE

LANGUAGE

Language is the choice of communication for the humankind.

It is nothing but sound vibrations structured and formed into patterns over centuries.

Every language creates a finite set of sound vibrations, be it a monosyllabic or multi-syllabic word.

AUM Is a classic example in this regard. If you say OM, it is monosyllabic. If you say A-U-M, it is tri-syllabic with respect to sound vibrations.

In Sanskrit, O is a diphthong formed by combining 'aa' and 'uu'.

AUM, as a chanting and as a mere prefix to all mantras is "Anahat Nadha" or the 'unstruck sound'

which is a typical sound which does not cause any obstruction in the oral cavity when it is said or chanted.

Every Faith has its own words, mantras, phrases and verses for chanting.

And the idea behind is they cause vibrations in our body and also form an Aura of sound vibrations around the individual.

As the scientists and researchers have found out, the entire existence of mankind is an amalgamation of sounds and the Universe is a manifestation of reverberations of energy.

Whenever one chants a mantra or a phrase or a verse, one can feel the vibrations a3 points in the body:

1. Vibrations around navel and abdominal area

2. Vibrations in and around the chest and throat areas

3. Vibrations in the forehead at a point between the two eyebrows.

The pause after the chanting followed by silence gives a meditation effect, Turiya, infinite consciousness

and brings in restfulness and energy.

So, if you have a habit of chanting, experience the recharge it does to your system.

Most Leaders/Champions have a rhythmic pattern of regular chanting of something of their considered choice.

It could be Faith related or a generic Positive Affirmation or a specific physical activity.

Be a CHAMPION. Behave like a CHAMPION.

THIRTY-SIX

MBD

MBO is Management By Objectives.

MBR is Management By Results.

MBD is Management By Dreaming, where Dreaming is an acronym meant for anyone aiming to accomplish something.

It is a simple step by step approach to succeed in studies, work, sports and arts and every other field.

Here is how MBD unfolds . . .

D reaming

D - Develop a vision, a goal. Without being ambitious no one is going to win.

d R eaming

R - Reinforce the vision after analysing it from different perspectives. A goal must be achievable.

"I will be President day after tomorrow " cannot be an achievable vision.

dr E aming

E - Ensure total, in fact 110% commitment to whatever you want to achieve.

dre A ming

A - Analyse the path to take including qualities, qualifications,tools and techniques.

drea M ing

M - Mobilize the required resources yourself because no one will be interested in this work.

dream I ng

I - Initiate action. Having identified what you want to achieve and mobilized resources, set the ball rolling.

dreami N g

N - Nullify obstacles. Once you start moving, hurdles might crop up and you must cross them one at a time.

dreamin G

G - Get going. Once you have nullified the hiccups, just move forward at full steam firing on all cylinders.

Champions dream big. Strive big. And achieve big.

Be a CHAMPION. Behave like a CHAMPION.

THIRTY-SEVEN

PAST AND PRESENT

Almost all gurus and acharyas of Hinduism, including the self-proclaimed ones,

differ in their explanation of many philosophies but converge in their opinion on one aspect of life and have total agreement.

It is this . . .

Our past consists of our actions. Our future consists of our hope.

Our past offers us experience. Our future unfolds with our Vision.

Our past teaches us life-lessons.Our future depends on our learnings.

Our past comes to our mind whether we worry or not.Our future unveils even whether we plan or not.

Our past is our KARMA.

Our future is our AASHA (desire).

Our NOW IS a Blessing.

Our NOW is a Present.

Our NOW is a Gift.

To give anything less than our BEST is to disrespect our GIFT.

Ordinary people seldom do justice in giving their best but they seldom fail to come up with excuses and seldom accept the results without complaining or whining and wailing.

CHAMPIONS don't stop with just giving their best to stay supreme, but they give their best and then a little more. As Sachin said after Mumbai Indians won the IPL 2017, "once a CHAMPION, always a CHAMPION."

Be a CHAMPION. Behave like a CHAMPION.

THIRTY-EIGHT

COLOURS AND HINDUISM

Every religion and faith has its own way of associating colours with emotions and assigning decorative values.

Hinduism which is attuned with nature and spiritual forms gives a signature importance to every colour.

GREEN represents life. Represents happiness. Represents stability. Colour of 4th Chakra Anahata.

YELLOW is the colour of learning, of knowledge, of generic peace and exuberance. Colour of 3rd Chakra Manipura.

WHITE depicts harmony and purity, the satva guna. White symbolises a sinless, self-sacrificing quality like a camphor and the ability to lead others. Colour of the 6th Chakra Ajna.

(There is a school of thought that says that Indigo is the colour of Ajna).

BLACK depicts tamas, inertia and ignorance. It also symbolises courage and heights of capabilities.

RED symbolises energy, passion, strength, resilience and such other rajas qualities. Also depicts purity and good omen. Colour of 1st Chakra Muladhara.

BLUE is the colour of the Creator. Colour of the protector. Colour of compassion.

Colour of valour, displayed if necessary. Colour of 5th Chakra Vishuddha.

ORANGE (Saffron is an accepted shade) is a sacred colour under Hinduism. It conveys denunciation, abstinence, holiness and the quest for enlightenment. Colour of 2nd Chakra Swadhisthana.

GOLDEN colour is very special and exclusive to Hinduism. Sundara Kanda in Ramayana mentions this colour while describing Hanuman (HAEMSHALB DEHAM - meaning body like Golden Mountain). It depicts humility despite the hugeness, modesty before almighty. Colour of the 7th Chakra Sahasra.

Now let us see The God or Goddess associated with a specific colour :

White -- Vinayaka

Yellow --- Lakshmi

Red -- Murugan

Black and White-- Shiva

Orange-- Brahma

Green and Red -- Sakthi

Blue – Vishnu

White -- Saraswathi

Saffron-- Iyappan.

Note: This analysis is from a spiritual standpoint. Therapy, architecture, healing, Vastu may all view colours differently.

THIRTY-NINE

SHAKESPEARE

If each of us ever could write down the names of leaders/ champions in the English literary field, the one name that would figure in everyone's list is that of WILLIAM SHAKESPEARE. The great genius is a monumental leader in English, not just as a playwright or poet but more as a significant contributor to the English language.

Right from the very beginning Shakespeare started to adopt a different style of writing scripts and dialogues, revolutionizing English plays, thereby revolutionizing the very language itself. He wrote an amazing 800,000 words in his plays alone and is credited with the glory of contributing some 20K new words for the English vocabulary. Phenomenal achievement, isn't it?

Shakespeare wrote some 35 plays and 150+ sonnets.

His plays have been translated into every living language and are being performed in some part of the world even as you are reading this. He is the most quoted English writer today even after over 450 years.

Ben Johnson famously said, "Shakespeare is not of an age but for all time" and went on to call him "The Sweet Swan of Avon." (Avon is the river flowing through Stratford where Shakespeare was born).

Our two most favourites of his plays are Merchant of Venice and Julius Caesar.

Our favourite sonnet is "No longer mourn for me when I am dead."

And there are several quotes of his that we love.

So, what are the leadership traits that Shakespeare has given to aspiring Champions?

1. Clarity of thought
2. Creativity (in integrating fiction with history)
3. Subject matter expertise
4. Analytical mind
5. Thinking for others (an astonishing 3750 characters in his plays)
6. Mastery over the Language
7. Kingliness in his demeanour
8. Professional integrity (never ever copied from any other author)
9. Energy flow (from himself to the readers)
10. Inspired, inspiring and will inspire 1000s of writers and poets.

What else do we need? As William Hazlitt, a well known literary critic said "If we wish to know the force of human genius we should read Shakespeare. If we wish to see the insignificance of human learning we can study his commentators."

Let's enjoy Shakespeare.

Let's admire Shakespeare.

Let's be inspired by Shakespeare.

Be a CHAMPION. Behave like a CHAMPION.

FORTY

God's Presence

One day, a man wanted to test the existence of God.

The man whispered, "God, speak to me" and a meadowlark sang, but the man did not hear.

So the man yelled, "God, SPEAK to me" and a thunder rolled across the sky, but the man didn't listen.

The man looked around and said, "God, let me see you" and a star shone brightly. But the man did not notice.

And the man shouted, "God, show me a miracle" and a new baby was born but the man did not know.

So the man cried out in despair, "Touch me God and let me know You are here"

Whereupon God reached down and touched the man.

But the man brushed the butterfly off and walked away saying "There is no God"

MORAL: Don't reject a blessing because it may not be packaged the way you expect.

FORTY-ONE

4F

As a Champion, when you build your gr8 career remember there will be people --

Who Will rate you. Who Will hate you.

Who Will shake you. Who Will break you.

Who Will outclass you. Who Will outlaw you.

Who Will appease you. Who Will abuse you.

Who will compliment you. Who will condemn you.

Who will trust you. Who will crush you.

Who will coax you. Who will hoax you.

Who will make you gleam. Who will make yo scream.

Who will smile at you. Who will sneer at you.

Who will harness you. Who will garnish you.

Whatever others do to you, remember you are a champion and you must behave like a champion at all times.

Remember the 4 Fs

Don't Fly.

Don't Freeze.

Don't Fight.

Just Face it.

Remain calm. Remain strong. Remain focused.

Continue to E X C E L.

Be a CHAMPION. Behave like a CHAMPION.

FORTY-TWO
The Pygmalion Effect

One quintessential quality that good Leaders/Champions possess is the unflinching confidence they place on their team or other members with them. They believe strongly that anyone can perform as good as themselves and keep pushing their limits.

Invariably, most team members respond positively and perform at a much higher plane than they themselves could have imagined. Pete Sampras won a few titles consecutively, saying that he "Did it for his coach," Tim Gullikson.

The great Australian legend Dennis Lillee after breaking his back was asked by a reporter "But you knew you were hurting yourself. Why did you not stop bowling?" Lillee nonchalantly replied "I will never say no when my captain (Ian Chappell) says I can do it. He gave me all the opportunity all these years. He believes in me. In my abilities. In my bowling. I will bowl if he says the team needs you to take a few wickets, even if it means I will break my back. Period."

Such is the power of this belief, the self-fulfilling prophecy.

In psychology this is called as the Pygmalion Effect.

It is named after a Greek mythological sculptor Pygmalion, who carved a statue, fell in love with it, and God gave life to the statue.

(The opposite of this is The GOLEM Effect which is expecting only lesser performance by others and they also perform in a substandard manner).

Leaders/Champions always have the Pygmalion Effect on their team perceiving a higher capability from them

and there sure is a correlation between their perception and the actual outcome.

So let's place trust on our team and co-beings that they can "Do it for us." And they will do it for us.

Leaders/Champions know very well that how we make others feel about themselves speak a lot about ourselves.

Be a CHAMPION. Behave like a CHAMPION.

FORTY-THREE
EFFICIENCY VS EXCELLENCE

Efficiency is ephemeral. Excellence is eternal.

Leaders/Champions are wonderful creatures when it comes to Optimizing Performance and reaching the peak of greatness with ease.

There is a science involved in the manner in which these stalwarts build their career brick by brick over five levels of performance.

1. ADHOC

Everyone in this world start with their basic capabilities and show their talent with one or two ADHOC performances. 20% of the people are happy with their 'flash in the pan" actions and stop at this level.

2. REPETITIVE

They then do the show again with REPETITIVE special acts and most of the people stop at this second level. 10% people become contented with their success and another 20% become arrogant about their so called repeated success and stop growing.

3. WELL DEFINED

The rest of the pack now move to the 3rd level where they are now a regular performer and start operating in a WELL-DEFINED AND DEMARCATED role. Success at this level triggers satisfactory under-performance and another 30% fade away after this level due to this.

4. PROLIFIC

Now the last 20% shows their consistency and give PROLIFIC PERFORMANCE. About10% at this level are clearly satisfied as they mistakenly feel that they are now solid performers who can never be overlooked. Most teams/families accept this and prolong the tenure of these people and the performers get stuck little short of greatness.

5. OPTIMIZED

The final 10% are the true Leaders/Champions who continue to unlearn, continue to learn new skills and most importantly measure their performance on a regular basis. They know that "You cannot improve what you don't measure. You don't want to measure what you don't improve".

This is the level where OPTIMIZATION of performance happens. So, very rarely some stars are born overnight.

Every Leader/Champion goes through the grind and it is their grit, determination and never-say-die spirit

which take them to where they belong, the summit of eminence.

Be a CHAMPION. Behave like a CHAMPION.

FORTY-FOUR

SYSTEMS THINKING

We will try and explain a rather difficult concept in as simple a manner as possible and feasible.

The human thought process is normally uni-focused, meaning looking at one path or one angle at a time.

Our thinking is sometimes parallel, sometimes logical and in some rare occasions, lateral.

Seldom will our thinking be holistic. Such holistic approach is the essence of SYSTEMS THINKING, as promulgated by Peter Senge, his narration, basically, is meant for the corporate world.

An organization works almost exactly like a well-run family. And Systems Thinking helps us to understand all the perspectives, all the aspects and all the effects of any matter or issue or problem.

Systems Thinking unravels the mystery inasmuch as it can bring in a near-wholesome thought process in the analysis of any issue. All inter-related segments are viewed and analysed before arriving at a conclusion.

Systems Thinking encompasses Logical, Parallel and Lateral thinking approaches.

Logical thinking is information oriented, exploratory, vertical and takes the individual 'deep into the box'.

Parallel thinking is concept oriented, inclusive, horizontal and takes individual 'in and around the box.'

Lateral Thinking is graphic, creative, expansive and takes individual 'out of the box.'

Systems Thinking ensures that we see an issue from all these 3 approaches.

Example -- Poser: Jency is not breathing through the nose.

Approaches and conclusions:

- Logical == Humans breathe through the nose. So Jency must be dead.
- Parallel == Humans breathe through the nose. So put Jency on a ventilator so that she can be alive.
- Lateral == Jency has learnt Aatmasidhi yoga and can control the breathing for a sustained period.

Systems Thinking looks from all angles and concludes that "There are other living beings which need not breathe through the nose. Jency could be a fish."

This all-pervading approach is the essence of Systems Thinking - of course, it is much wider than this and Peter Senge has elucidated several guiding principles.

It is today extensively used in education, the medical field and in financial, production, marketing and human resources management.

There are sports coaches who are putting it into action to analyse an individual or team performance.

As Champions, we can successfully use the concept in our professional life and in the domestic circuit as well.

Be a CHAMPION. Behave like a CHAMPION.

FORTY-FIVE

EMOTIONAL WELLNESS

Kenopanishad says "NACHET AVADEET MAHATO VINASHYATHI" . . .

. . . Not realising this truth is a great loss.

One such truth is being undisturbed or unperturbed by the flood of emotions that every one experiences now and then in life.

Psychologists call this "Emotional Wellness."

The teeth-grinding determination to excel of the Sprezzeturans is built on the strong premise of Emotional Wellness. (Also referred as EI-Emotional Intelligence or EQ-Emotional Quotient).

Both EI and EQ are more scientific in their approaches and Emotional Wellness is more from a spiritual and practical angle.

Leaders/Champions normally enjoy a healthy state of Emotional Wellness and successfully sustain it for most part of their career and life. Not that they don't emote.

Of course they do, sometimes much more outwardly than normal, but they 'are aware' of what they are doing.

It is the state of "shuddha samkit," meaning a pure blessed state of self-realization, which is the core of Emotional Wellness.

How do the Leaders/Champions maintain their Emotional Wellness?

• They compulsively take their attention away from brooding and painful thoughts

• Their resilience after a failure or rejection is because they rediscover their self-worth

• They rekindle their passion every time they feel down and dejected

• They spend their disposable-freetime in relaxing, comforting, refreshing, and at times exciting pursuits

• They sound, look and act confident at all times especially when the chips are down

• They are ever thankful to every one who has contributed to their present stature

• They are modestly proud about themselves and their achievements

• They respect others for what they are and never strive to correct others unless the recipients are CLOSE to them

• They have a Vision which has been worded into a Mission followed by an action plan and they use all this to spring back from a failure or rejection

Be a CHAMPION. Behave like a CHAMPION.

FORTY-SIX

MUSIC AND CHAMPIONISM

For several centuries people have been judging a Leader/ Champion based on the arena he/she is performing.

It is not right at all. Let's analyse this scenario with the analogy of different types of music, focusing on Carnatic, Hindustani and Western music.

All 3 types use tonal quality and pitch as the base. A singer or instrumentalist normally journeys on the same pitch throughout the rendering in all 3 forms and at rare times takes a higher or lower octave to establish the range.

The way melody (tune) develops is a defining characteristic of each system.

Carnatic is sahithyam (song-lyrics) bound and the melody is the traditionally followed tune in the same raga and tala handed down generation after generation.

Creativity is applied to elaborate the raga and the swaras with wonderful variations called "gamagam."

Hindustani is Raga based. For the same lyrics a different raga and its movements (prayogam) and different talas can be used.

In Western, the singer or instrumentalist can use a different melody for the lyrics and sometimes even alter the lyrics, leave alone the rhythm.

Chord shifts as an accompanying instrument ("chords") is unique to Western.

Accompanying instruments in both Carnatic and Hindustani both have to 'follow' the lead artist

and are assigned 'personal' time to exhibit their talents.

Employing 'seconds' in singing or in background score, where a secondary tune accompanies the main so as to embellish the latter is again very exclusive to Western.

These two aspects of Western are inherently etched in Indian filmy music.

Though accompaniments, duets and jugalbandhis are used extensively in both Carnatic and Hindustani, there is no practice of a secondary tune. The accompanying tone will only accentuate the original by rendering the same tune.

As for the rhythm, Carnatic has over 100 talas and has numerous permutations with different counts for each timing stroke ('Sethusra, Thisra nadais).

Hindustani has lesser number of talas and the emphasis is more on the speed (kala parimanam).

Western has very few types with the emphasis on pure rhythmic flow and timing (2-4, 4-4, 6-8, and so on).

The comparison is endless as each form is an ocean by itself and I haven't touched even a droplet.

A very skeletal outline is what I have attempted.

Whatever be the type, music is divine.

Every form is deep and WIDER. Every type is a mystic. Every format enthralls the listener.

Similarly, leaders are of several types, be it in arts, sports, corporate or domestic field.

If you dissect a rose, some petals may remain but that is not rose.

If you further crush the petals we may get some chemicals but that is not rose again.

A rose must be smelt, admired and enjoyed.

In the same breadth, a CHAMPION is a Champion and we must not dissect the spirit but admire and enjoy the experience a

CHAMPION gives us.

FORTY-SEVEN

LISTENING

3 people were travelling in a bus in London. The bus stopped at one place.

"Is this Wembley?" The first man asked.

"Certainly not. Today is Thursday," said the second man.

"So am I. Let's go for a drink," pitched in the third guy.

The first person had asked about the place he had to get down.

The second was thinking about the day of the week.

And the third was thirsty.

MORAL of the incident:

We hear what we want to hear.

We listen what we want to listen to.

Listening is the most critical element of communication.

Most things can be conveyed only with the help of the listener.

And if we are the ones listening how well do we listen becomes imperative.

In Hinduism, all the sruthis and smiritis, ithikasas and puranas all have been handed down generation after generation for 1000s of years only through listening (shravanam).

We spend years learning how to read and write but not even a single class on listening, the much over looked communication skill.

Hearing is not listening. Hearing is just allowing the sound vibrations to enter the ears but listening is understanding what is being stated. And it is a people-skill rather than a communication skill.

A good listener is always accepted as a great conversationalist.

Good Leaders/Champions have a "Listening Presence," a quality that keeps them abreast of their people's feelings, ideas and thought process.

They maintain eye contact, observe the posture and gesture of the person to whom they are listening, rephrase their understanding before speaking their own views.

We have formed the mnemonic MASTER to exactly do what a Leader/Champion does.

The content, context, clarity, speed of communication, other distractions, our own thoughts-flow, have all to be taken into account.

Now to MASTER . . .

M

MAINTAIN - Maintain eye contact and attention to what is being said.

A

(be) ACTIVE - we must deploy Active Listening, meaning responsive listening (nodding, monosyllabic acknowledgement etc).

S

SUSTAIN - Sustain total interest in the comm-process.

T

TARGET - Target the goal or atleast the end of the communication. Do not interrupt unless it is a leading query.

E

ELIMINATE - Eliminating all filters and judgemental opinions is a must.

R

RECALL - Rephrase and recall atleast once in order to remember.

Remember the acronym MASTER and we can master the art of listening as effectively as a Champion.

Be a CHAMPION. Behave like a CHAMPION.

FORTY-EIGHT

KARMA

"In a Worldless
Timeless
Lightless
Great Emptiness
... Lord Brahma broods"

--- Rabindranath Tagore

☆☆☆☆☆☆☆☆☆☆☆☆☆

How can the suffering of a just-born child be linked to what the child could have done in this birth? How can we explain why a very noble person who had never done any harm to anyone suffer from a terminal illness like cancer?

How can we explain why a person, notorious for his vices, lives a king-like life, unaffected by any of the wrongs?

Saints and Mahaans have strongly reiterated that the suffering or joyfulness one goes through in one's life time is not the resultant effect of what one did earlier in one's present life.

It is the result of what one did earlier in his previous birth or births.

The actions of this birth bear their results in the next births only.

KARMA is explained in detail in both Hinduism and Buddhism (Cetenà).

The philosophy of KARMA elucidates principles of cause and effect, where intent and actions of an individual (cause) influence the future of that individual (effect).

KARMA is of 3 types.

Prarabdha, Sanchita and Agami or Kriyamana.

Prarabdha is the past karma that has already unfolded and responsible for the present body and the experience.

Sanchita is also karma from the past but waiting to unfold. Sometimes may unfold in the present and some in the next births.

Agami is those present actions that shall result in effects in future janmas.

Prarabdha is fructified past karma.

Sanchita is past karma waiting to fructify.

Agami is current karma leading to the future where it will fructify.

In Vedantic works, there is a plethora of explanations for KARMA, all of them concluding that a divine power is the guiding force and therefore, prayers is the only recourse.

Sankara mentions this to a distinct effect in his Bhaja Govindham verse "punarabi jananam punarabi maranam."

And Kaviyarasar Kannadasan gives his translation of that verse in a Virutham form:

"Thai vayitrile pirandhu , Than irandhu
Meendum meendum, thai vayitrile pirakiren.
Dharanikule pirandhu
Vanvelikule midhandhu
Dharanikule pirakiren.
Oiviladha en pirappu
Meendum meendum yaar poruppu
Unnai andri veru kangilen
Oorilulla jeevanukku
Nee kotutha vazhkai endru
Unnidathil ennai vaikiren."

"FAITH is the Bird
that feels the light
when the Dawn is
still Dark."

---- Rabindranath Tagore

FORTY-NINE

AFFLUENCE VS AFFORDABILITY

Right through history two different corporates in the same field but with two tangentially different ideology have emerged as world leaders in their respective industries.

One set caters to the Affluent while the other to Affordable buyers.

Some examples of such pairs: (a striking point here is, there are no Indian companies mainly because Indian corporates do not specialise for only one segment of clientele).

Watches: 1. ROLEX and 2. CITIZEN.

Luxury Cars: 1. ROLLS ROYCE and 2. MERCEDES.

Hotels: 1. MARRIOTT and 2. HOLIDAY INN.

Aircrafts: 1. BOEING and 2. AIRBUS.

PCs and Software: 1. APPLE and 2. MICROSOFT.

Apparel: 1. LOIUS PHILIP and 2. PETER ENGLAND.

Electronic Keyboards: 1. YAMAHA and 2. CASIO.

Tablets and Laptops: 1. TOSHIBA and 2. DELL.

Passenger Cars: 1. TOYOTA and 2. HYUNDAI.

Mobile Phones: 1. APPLE and 2. SAMSUNG.

Both sets of the big names have got a Brandname, Enjoy huge patronage, Make large profits, and are led and managed by successful LEADERS.

So, what else are the differentiators?

The first named companies in every category

• Built their capability through absolute creativity.

• Made a dearer product or service by intentionally producing less.

• Add-ons and extra services all built into the ONE-PRICE-BUT-WHOLESOME Experience.

• Created an artificial "want" with a perfectly built "NEW idea for the ELITE" (everyone WANTS it) and made the waiting a little longer.

• Buyers / Users felt great as they became PROUD owners/users.

• Everything is about a high level of quality and innovation.

• Profits maximized with a super-hi price structure.

All the names listed second in each category above

• Built their capabilities through improvisations.

• Made MORE products and WIDER reach of consumers.

• Prices were for the "Base" product and "ADD-ONS" were charged extra. (But ancillary industries flourished).

• Created an artificial DEMAND-SUPPLY magic (everyone NEEDS it) and waiting time was considerably less.

• Buyers/Users became "HAPPY" that they have all the features that are there in the 'bigger' brand.

• Quality took a backseat and innovation was replaced with improvisation.

• Profits maximized with VOLUME of sales.

Both sets of corporates are extremely successful leaders despite adhering to a reasonably diagonally opposite approaches.

It doesn't matter what you do as long as you do it right.

Excellence is not a destination but a journey.

It is the spirit with which we act that puts the seal of beauty upon the journey of excellence.

These corporates have peaked with their spirit to Excel.

Let's learn from their stories.

Be a CHAMPION. Behave like a CHAMPION.

FIFTY

ASSERTIVENESS

In general one's behaviour can fall into one of the 3 types, Passive, Aggressive and Assertive.

Everyone wants to be Assertive in behaviour, action and communication.

Assertiveness means to affirm positively, strongly and assuredly.

A PASSIVE person's

- appearance will be apprehensive,
- eye contact will be minimal,
- posture will be collapsed,
- facial expression will be dull/sad,
- hands will be limp,
- voice will be hesitant and
- respect for others will be too much.
- They allow others to abuse or manipulate their own personal boundaries.

An AGGRESSIVE person's

- appearance will be tense,
- eye contact will be agitated,
- posture will be domineering,
- facial expression will be hard and serious,
- hands will be hyperactive,
- voice will be unnecessarily loud and
- respect for others will be almost absent.

• They don't have any respect for others' boundaries.

An ASSERTIVE person's

• appearance will be relaxed,
• eye contact will be direct,
• posture will be upright/elegant,
• facial expression will be responsive,
• hands will be casual,
• voice will be confident and
• respect for others will be fully present.
• They don't allow any abuse of their own boundaries but at the same time never tread on others' boundaries.
• They don't repress their feelings but have great control over their anger and other emotions.

Champions always appear to be somehow assertive at all times. They may appear humble and yet they will be assertive to the core. They are relaxed, responsive and confident in their actions.

Be a CHAMPION. Behave like a CHAMPION.

FIFTY-ONE
DAILY REMINDERS

SMILE

"Never let the world change your smile.

Always let your smile change the world."

EXCELLENCE

What does EXCELLENCE mean to you?

Courage is not mere absence of fear but conquest of fear.

Quality is not mere absence of defects but presence of a tangible value.

Success is not mere absence of failure but overcoming adversity against all odd

Excellence is not mere absence of mediocrity but a combo of passion, talent and commitment

With EXCELLENCE, success becomes incidental.

The trenchant craving for EXCELLENCE is actually a SEQUEL to an unswerving SINGLENESS of what you want to accomplish.

LUCK

Two major sports with billions of fans all over the world – Cricket and Wimbledon – have both taught us that:

LUCK DOESN'T HAPPEN to you.

You MAKE LUCK TO HAPPEN

- your preparedness takes you to meet the opportunities and if you meet those opportunities for a favourable result, your potential takes you to luck and....

You MAKE LUCK HAPPEN and.... You WIN.

WHO WE ARE

When someone CRITICIZES you, it doesn't define who you are. It establishes WHO THEY ARE.

When you JUDGE someone, it doesn't define who they are. It establishes WHO YOU ARE.

PRETTY

Let us boldly focus on being PRETTY.

YES.

Let's focus on being . . . .

PRETTY kind.

PRETTY strong.

PRETTY smart."

LESSONS

After going through a tough time, ***FORGET*** what ***HURT*** you but

NEVER FORGET what it ***TAUGHT*** you.

CHAMPIONS

A *CHAMPION* has . . . .

COMPASSION about the PAST,

COURAGE about the PRESENT and
CONVICTION about the FUTURE.

SUCCESS

"A *DREAM* written down with a clear date becomes a *GOAL* .
A *GOAL* broken down into solid steps becomes a *PLAN* .
A *PLAN* backed by effective action becomes a *SUCCESS."*

HOPE - TRUST - FAITH

HOPE is

When everything is going bad, believing that SOMETHING good is out there over the horizon.

TRUST is

When everything is going bad, believing that a PARTICULAR PERSON will help you out of the problem.

FAITH is

When everything is going bad, believing that THE SUPREME POWER will bring you WHAT is BETTER for you.

DIGNITY

CHARITY is highlighted by PURITY of the man
BREVITY is highlighted by CLARITY of the thought
DIGNITY is highlighted by HUMILITY of the heart

Printed by Libri Plureos GmbH in Hamburg,
Germany